MYSTERIES OF SCIENCE

THE BERMUDA TRIANGLE

THE UNSOLVED MYSTERY

BY CONNIE COLWELL MILLER

Reading Consultant:
Barbara J. Fox
Reading Specialist
North Carolina State University

Content Consultant:
Gian J. Quasar
Author/Historian
www.bermuda-triangle.org

Capstone
press

Mankato, Minnesota

Blazers is published by Capstone Press,
151 Good Counsel Drive, P.O. Box 669, Mankato, Minnesota 56002.
www.capstonepress.com

Library of Congress Cataloging-in-Publication Data
Miller, Connie Colwell, 1976–
 The Bermuda Triangle: the unsolved mystery/by Connie Colwell Miller.
 p. cm. — (Blazers. Mysteries of science)
 Includes bibliographical references and index.
 Summary: "Presents the legend of the Bermuda Triangle, including current theories and
famous examples" — Provided by publisher.
 ISBN-13: 978-1-4296-2330-8 (hardcover)
 ISBN-10: 1-4296-2330-6 (hardcover)
 1. Bermuda Triangle — Juvenile literature. I. Title. II. Series.
G558.M55 2009
001.94 — dc22   2008028701

Editorial Credits
Lori Shores, editor; Alison Thiele, designer; Marcie Spence, photo researcher

Photo Credits
Alamy/MasPix, 24–25
AP Images/NOAA, File, cover, 20–21
Capstone Press/Danielle Ceminsky, 11
Corbis/Bettmann, 6–7, 22–23; George Hall, 4–5; Horace Bristol, 12–13
Fortean Picture Library, 26–27
Getty Images Inc./Norbert Wu, 8–9; Suk-Heui Park, 28–29
Library of Congress, 10
Shutterstock/Lowell Sannes, 14–15; Marilyn Volan, grunge background (throughout);
 Matsonashvili Mikhail, 16–17; Maugli, 18–19 (background); rgbspace, (paper art element) 3,
 19; Shmeliova Natalia, 18 (paper art element)

1 2 3 4 5 6 14 13 12 11 10 09

TABLE OF CONTENTS

CHAPTERS

FEATURES

MISSING

Air traffic controllers in Florida watched their **radar** screens on October 31, 1991. They were guiding John Verdi's jet.

radar — a device that uses radio waves to track the location of objects

Verdi asked the controllers if he could fly higher. The controllers watched the **blip** on the screen.

blip — a spot of light on a radar screen that shows the location of an object

John Verdi was flying a Grumman
Cougar Jet similar to this one.

Verdi's jet might be at the bottom of the ocean.

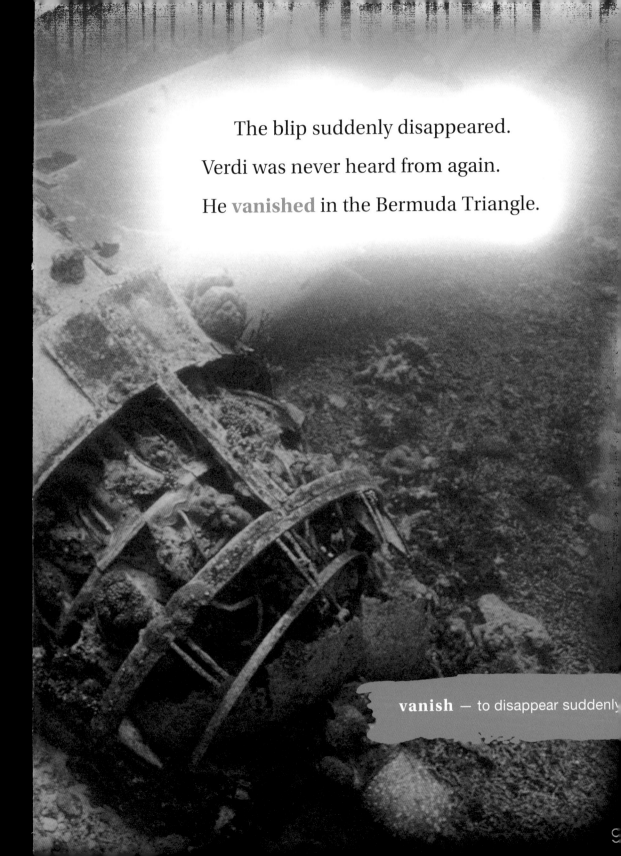

The blip suddenly disappeared.

Verdi was never heard from again.

He **vanished** in the Bermuda Triangle.

vanish — to disappear suddenly

THE BERMUDA TRIANGLE

The Bermuda Triangle is an area of the Atlantic Ocean. The points of the triangle are Bermuda, Puerto Rico, and Miami, Florida.

A Navy supply ship, the USS *Cyclops*, disappeared in the Bermuda Triangle in 1918.

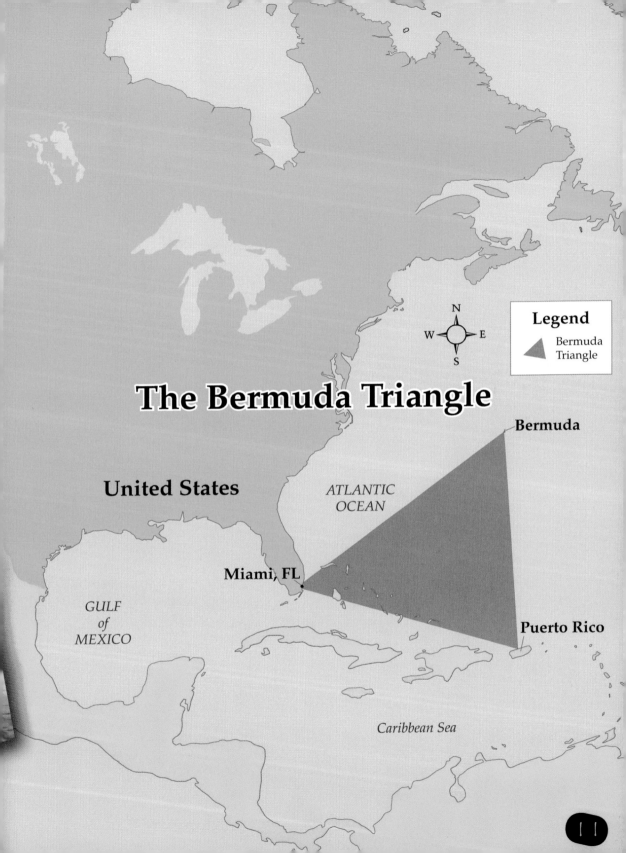

The Bermuda Triangle

Legend
Bermuda Triangle

Bermuda

United States

ATLANTIC OCEAN

Miami, FL

Puerto Rico

GULF of MEXICO

Caribbean Sea

Hundreds of boats and planes have been lost in the Bermuda Triangle since 1940. No one knows what happened to them.

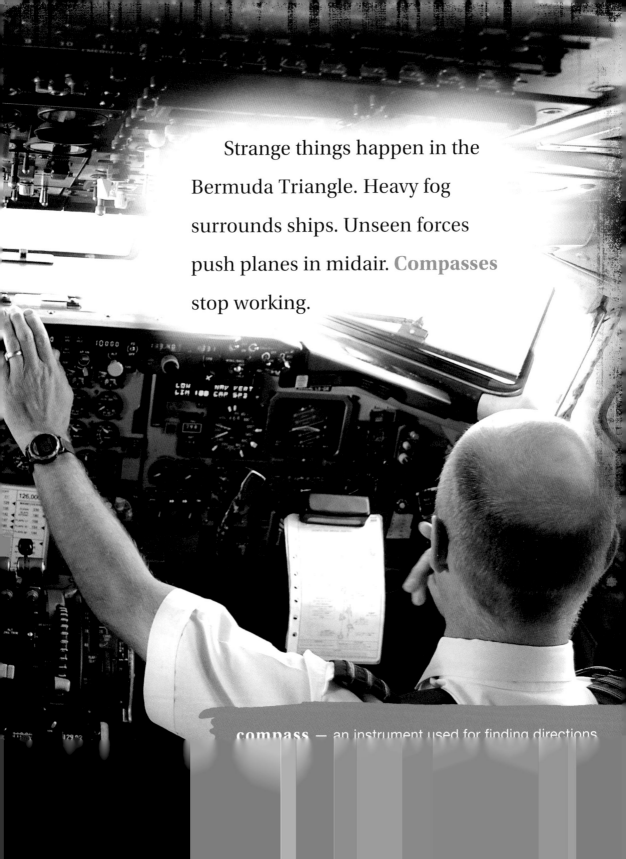

Strange things happen in the Bermuda Triangle. Heavy fog surrounds ships. Unseen forces push planes in midair. **Compasses** stop working.

compass — an instrument used for finding directions

Some disappearances are hard to explain. Most missing captains and pilots were skilled and in good health. Many planes and ships have disappeared in good weather.

TRIANGLE FACT

About 20 boats disappear in the Bermuda Triangle every year.

FAMOUS EXPERIENCES

▲ In 1945, Flight 19 took off on a training mission. An hour after takeoff, the leader reported that their compasses weren't working. All five U.S. Navy torpedo planes went missing.

▲ Charles Lindbergh flew through a strange fog in the Bermuda Triangle in 1928. When the fog cleared, Lindbergh noticed that he had flown farther than his fuel supply should have allowed.

▲ The cargo ship *Marine Sulphur Queen* disappeared in the Bermuda Triangle in 1963. Rescue teams searched for the crew for 19 days. But the crew of 39 men was never found.

▲ In 1966, Captain Don Henry and his crew were towing a ship to Miami, Florida. Suddenly, the compass needle started to spin and the power failed. A thick fog hid the ship they were pulling. The crew members were safe, but they never forgot what happened.

WHAT HAPPENS IN THE TRIANGLE?

Scientists study what happens in the Bermuda Triangle. Some scientists think a **magnetic field** causes radios and compasses to fail. People then get lost.

magnetic field — an area of moving electrical currents that affects other objects

Other scientists say storms are to blame. Ships that get caught in sudden storms could sink. Planes could crash.

TRIANGLE
FACT

Most of the time, searchers
find no bodies or wreckage
in the Bermuda Triangle.

TRIANGLE FACT

Some people believe power sources from a mythical sunken city called Atlantis are to blame.

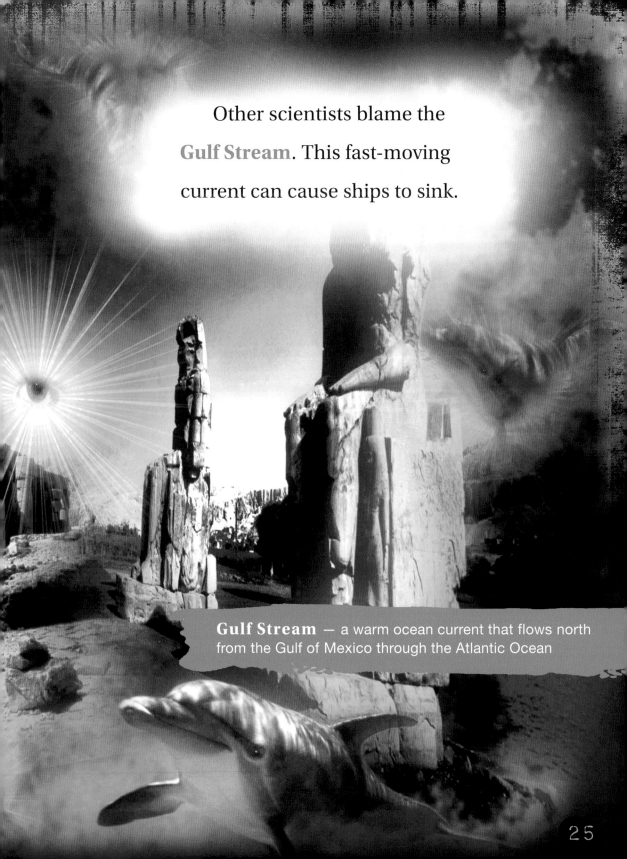

Other scientists blame the **Gulf Stream**. This fast-moving current can cause ships to sink.

Gulf Stream — a warm ocean current that flows north from the Gulf of Mexico through the Atlantic Ocean

ANYTHING IS POSSIBLE

Many people think something **supernatural** is happening. Some say alien spaceships snatch up planes and ships from the triangle.

supernatural — something that cannot be given an ordinary explanation

TRIANGLE FACT

In the 1977 film *Close Encounters of the Third Kind*, aliens kidnap people from the Bermuda Triangle.

What is happening in the Bermuda Triangle? Maybe someday scientists will find the answers.

TRIANGLE FACT

The Bermuda Triangle is sometimes called the Devil's Triangle.

GLOSSARY

blip (BLIP) — a spot of light on a radar screen that shows the location of an object

compass (KUHM-puhs) — an instrument used for finding directions

Gulf Stream (GUHLF STREEM) — a warm ocean current that flows north from the Gulf of Mexico through the Atlantic Ocean

magnetic field (mag-NET-ic FEELD) — an area of moving electrical currents that affects other objects

mythical (MITH-i-kuhl) — imaginary or possibly not real

radar (RAY-dar) — a device that uses radio waves to track the location of objects

supernatural (soo-pur-NACH-ur-uhl) — something that cannot be given an ordinary explanation

vanish (VAN-ish) — to disappear suddenly

wreckage (REK-ij) — the broken remains of a plane or ship that has crashed

READ MORE

Hamilton, Sue. *The Bermuda Triangle.* Unsolved Mysteries. Edina, Minn.: ABDO, 2008.

Oxlade, Chris. *The Mystery of the Bermuda Triangle.* Can Science Solve? Chicago: Heinemann, 2006.

West, David. *The Bermuda Triangle: Strange Happenings at Sea.* Graphic Mysteries. New York: Rosen, 2006.

INTERNET SITES

FactHound offers a safe, fun way to find educator-approved Internet sites related to this book.

Here's what you do:

1. Visit *www.facthound.com*
2. Choose your grade level.
3. Begin your search.

This book's ID number is 9781429623308.

FactHound will fetch the best sites for you!

INDEX